INDIVIDUAL EMPOWERMENT

A WAY TO A BETTER FUTURE

Inquiries and Book Orders should be addressed to:

Frangi Publishing

ISBN: 978-1-961416-22-2 (sc)
ISBN: 978-1-961416-24-6 (hc)
ISBN: 978-1-961416-23-9 (ebk)

INDIVIDUAL EMPOWERMENT

A WAY TO A BETTER FUTURE

ERIC GRIBBLE

CONTENTS

Preface............................... ix

Chapter 1: Innovation, Lateral Thinking,
and Competition 1

Chapter 2: Emails to the Treasurer 7

Chapter 3: Protectionism and risk.................17

Chapter 4: Decentralisation, Free Speech,
and Self-Esteem 27

Chapter 5: Small Government and Tax.............36

Chapter 6: Social Structure, Health,
Education, and Law and
Order Social Structure.................48

Chapter 7: Global Warming 60

Chapter 8: The Future 80

Conclusion 87

Bibliography 93

References 95

This book is dedicated to my late wife, Kaye. Kaye gave me great encouragement and support. Despite a long illness, she continued working and battling for young people. As a child health nurse, she understood and practised the principle of mentoring young teenage mothers. Kaye was the most inspirational, compassionate, self-sacrificing, and bravest person I have known, and I miss her a lot.

Most people believe there is a better way of doing things. We laughed at ourselves; we laughed at the BBC series *Yes, Minister* as we knew it was reality. We all bemoan big government wastage and criticise unfair taxes and stupid regulations. The problem is that big government has gradually sneaked upon us. We need to look at the total picture rather than small components if society is to be restructured. Reform of our society and its structures is the next big step Australia needs to take. It is my hope that this book will promote open discussion, debate, and ultimately, reform.

I've had an uneasy feeling for some time now. The mood of optimism we once had seems to have gone. Every new project, every new technology, seems to be greeted with a barrage of opposition. There is a clamour for more and more regulation to fix every perceived wrong. There is a feeling of hopelessness, an unsaid belief that our species is heading for calamity through overuse of resources, pollution, and destructive climate change. The growth of government and taxes has been the ongoing trend, with individuals looking to the government for every solution rather than relying on themselves. We seem to have lost our basic values. We have foregone the principles of personal empowerment and personal responsibility, of self-reliance.

Let us be optimistic. Technology is the solution, and I wish to share that optimism by demonstrating an alternative path for Australia and the world.

CHAPTER 1

INNOVATION, LATERAL THINKING, AND COMPETITION

Innovation drives economies. Innovators are individuals who step out from the crowd, who dare to be different. Economies that are successful relative to other economies are generally those that are more innovative. All products go through a lifecycle. The *start-up* or *development phase* of a new product/service costs money. Then, once on the market, the monopoly position of the business enables high profitability. The *maturity phase* is when many begin manufacturing the product locally and overseas, resulting in profits dropping to a mere subsistence level due to competition. Ultimately, the product may be superseded by further innovation. If an economy is constantly producing products that have not reached the maturity phase, that economy will prosper.

Thinking innovatively is lateral thinking. Lateral thinking is breaking away from the pattern that is leading in a definite direction.

Innovation and new startups flourish in an environment where there are sources of finance (venture capital), educational facilities, efficient infrastructure, limited regulations, equal opportunity (level playing field), low taxes, free trade, support from large corporations and encouragement and support from society.

Entrepreneurs need to be innovative, need to be market researchers and have management ability.

Luck versus Entrepreneurship

Luck = where *expectations* meet up with *opportunities*.

Opportunities are everywhere and are already there—you can only increase expectations. But an unprepared mind cannot see opportunities.

I once worked with a man who had been a paratrooper in a Highland Regiment. He was based in Scotland, however, when on leave would take the train to London. Three of them would buy one ticket. When the conductor was due to do his rounds, all three would go into the toilet. The conductor would knock on the door, and the ticket would be passed over the top. It would be clipped and handed back. This worked twice, however the third time, the ticket did not come back. It must have been another Scotsman after a free ticket. Scotsmen do have a reputation for being innovative and frugal.

It appears to me that analytical thinkers tend to be lateral thinkers. This could go a long way towards explaining why innovation comes from the sciences; there has been little evolution in our institutions. Lawyers and accountants have memorized case law and legislation. All their learning is procedure-based, following the rulebook. They are administrators; the idea that the rulebook should be torn up is outside their perception. Engineers, scientists, physicists, and mathematicians think analytically and laterally.

If you believe in Darwinism, you will believe that the human species evolves backwards as the natural selection process has stopped (a subject people understandably do not wish to talk about). Our society also evolves the same way, in part due to competition and natural selection among producers and service providers. There is a difference with biological evolution; genetic mutation and variation result in new pathways branching from existing pathways, whereas, in social and technological evolution, innovation can come from nowhere and completely bypass (leapfrog) existing pathways.

Existing products and services can become redundant pathways when a new concept bypasses them. Three examples are mainframe computers (largely replaced by desktops/laptops, remember IBM's dominance), film processing (largely replaced by digital imaging), and typing pools.

New technology cannot be predicted; who knows what may be forming in someone's head somewhere in the world right now? It comes at us from totally unexpected quarters. Who could have foreseen the internet forty years ago? Who could have foreseen the possible redundancy of the rocket industry as a means of reaching space (will be explained later in the book)? It has regularly been stated that technology is going to its limits; this is simply because new technology cannot be envisaged by everyone except those working on it till it becomes public.

The failing of government is that no individual or organisation can foresee the future. No individual or organisation can predict or control all the components, price changes, scarcity, etc., that go into a manufactured product. No individual or organisation can predict consumer preference now and into the future. Because of the millions of interactions within the private sector, the thousands of ideas the marketplace is testing, no individual or organisation can determine what may become a redundant pathway. Only the free market and price mechanism can constantly test products, ideas, and services.

A certain amount of bankruptcy is the market's way of weeding out both inefficiency and failed ideas. Although heartbreaking and soul-destroying for those involved, a small amount of bankruptcy is part of a healthy economy and frees up resources.

When governments try to pick winners and losers through tariff protection, subsidies, tax breaks and grants, they invariably get it wrong. Low taxes and a level playing field allows for the effective operation of the price mechanism. This model allows new wealth-creating products to flourish, leading to a more prosperous, innovative, exciting society.

Private sector enterprises in a competitive environment need to be courteous and responsive to their customers' needs. The reverse is true of an organization (private or government) in a monopoly. State-owned organisations tend to be monopolies. How often do people encounter uncooperative, surly, rude officials? A person with a similar attitude running a small business in a competitive environment would not survive.

Competition provides the outside force for constant improvements in efficiency, product differentiation, and service. Competing firms must constantly try to maintain or increase market share through price and quality. They constantly try to obtain a short-lived monopoly edge over their competitors through product improvement and differentiation. Competition helps drive innovation.

Monopolies take away consumer freedom of choice. The pressure is removed, and they adopt a take-it-or-leave-it attitude. Monopolies can compensate for inefficiencies by reducing payouts to producers and increasing charges to captive consumers and service users. Government services are generally in an uncompetitive monopoly situation. This is a reason for splitting up many of these services and placing them into the private sector. Also, strong competition legislation is needed, enabling the splitting up of private-sector monopolies and oligopolies.

A good example is the oligopoly of the two major supermarket chains in Australia. Their policy has become to avoid using small producers and to only deal with large distributors and suppliers. How can small innovative producers grow and become successful in such an environment? The home-brand policy, and giving large home-brand suppliers an advantage, take away product differentiation. It stifles innovation, ultimately reducing consumer choice (home branding should be illegal at the retail level if the retailer is not the producer). A good competition law would result in these two supermarket chains being split into about six chains. It would also ensure that there was no collusion between these retailers.

Bankruptcy is a part of a healthy competitive economy (it is better if entrepreneurs can cut their losses and bail out before they lose everything). The private businessperson can lose everything. Bankruptcy is the market's way of efficiently allocating resources.

Nothing, however, could be more devastating for the entrepreneur involved. Society needs to recognize the role and risk entrepreneurs take on. Some of the world's most successful entrepreneurs have been through bankruptcy before achieving success. When you never make mistakes, you never make anything (those who do nothing don't make mistakes). It is easy for those who never make anything to criticise. Entrepreneurs need friends when things go wrong; a friend is someone with whom you can be weak.

CHAPTER 2

EMAILS TO THE TREASURER

In early 2009, I exercised my freedom of speech and sent two emails to the then Treasurer of Australia, The Right Honorable Wayne Swan. The two emails are as follows.

Sent on 24 January 2009.

To: Mr Wayne Swan

Re: The current economic decline

One concern is that there will be a greater than normal number of receiverships and bankruptcies. The problem is that there is a domino effect in that perfectly viable businesses often end up in strife simply because they have supplied to and are owed by a business that has failed. In such a situation, the tax office will grab what is owed to the government ahead of unsecured creditors. My argument is that the government is simply a service provider (except that parliament is elected and makes the laws we live by). Small businesses are less able to cope with an unexpected and undeserved loss of income than the government. Therefore, I am proposing that the tax office (government) be placed either on the same level or below unsecured creditors in the event of a bankruptcy. This step will be a small step towards improving the private sector's stability and be a step forward in recognising the importance of the small business sector.

Another concern that I have is first home grants to first time new homebuyers. The housing boom has been the main reason for Australia's high level of international liabilities. Banks have borrowed abroad and lent to homebuyers. Homes do not generate income, but interest still needs to be paid. I believe it is a good thing for people to own and have pride in their own house. The problem is that an excessive amount has been invested in non-productive housing in recent years. It is the productive sector that needs stimulating, not the house construction industry. Balance is needed.

I have had an interesting book, *The Great Boom Ahead* by Harry S. Dent, MBA, on my shelf for many years. Published in 1993, he accurately predicted the stock market and US economic boom through the 1990s and early 2000s. He also predicted recession (which did occur and was called the Asian Crisis). He also predicted a major recession lasting ten years and up to 15 per cent unemployment in the United States from 2009 onward and advised people to get out of stocks from 2007 onwards.

How did he make these predictions? His predictions are based solely on population demographics. There is a baby boom bubble in the states, and as it ages, its spending behaviour alters (e.g., retirees no longer purchase houses). It is an interesting concept not considered by traditional economists.

Finally, it appears that the recent economic stimulus package has been saved rather than spent (counterproductive), reinforcing my belief that it is the supply side of the economy that needs stimulating. It is new and differentiated goods (the fruits of innovation) coming onto the market that stimulate demand. Below is a copy of the previous email I sent. (Sent on 20th Oct 2008).

I have concerns regarding the stimulus package introduced in response to the global credit crisis. A problem that OECD nations face is a large trade deficit. This suggests an imbalance between supply and demand. The OECD supply needs to increase, and consumption needs to increase in surplus nations such as China and the Middle East (and other surplus nations). Politicians have focused on the demand side of the equation. Low-income family grants and housing assistance will increase the consumption of imported goods and stimulate the housing sector. The problem is that long term productive capacity and the export sector needs to grow. Reducing the upper tax bracket also stimulates demand and consumption, demand for and consumption of factors of production (construction of new factories, consumption of inputs like fertilizer). Business expansion trickles down as new jobs and increased wages.

Expenditure on infrastructure only makes sense if there is a clear need if roads are so run down that there is a cost due to delays if there is a forecast electricity shortage etc. There needs to be a cost-benefit analysis on this type of spending. The price mechanism is the best way of efficiently allocating resources; unfortunately, infrastructure spending often occurs outside of the market's scrutiny and at the whim of politicians and public servants.

A feature of OECD economies has become a large government. In the immediate post war period, average government revenue was in the vicinity of 20 per cent. It is now closer to 40 per cent. So, itIt is hardly surprising OECD economies are stagnating relative to the amazing growth occurring in China.

The following are Quotes from *Wealth and Poverty* by George Gilder (Institute for Contemporary Studies, California). Note: he uses the term Liberal in the American sense.

"The source of the gifts of capitalism is the supply side of the economy. In the capitalist economies of the West, this simple recognition is the core of all successful economic policy. It is a principle sometime as obscure to conservatives, with their often excessive preoccupation with the statistics of money and deficit spending, as it is to liberals, with their obsession for aggregate demand and consumer spending".

"The problem is that demand, like public opinion, does not exist in any very definite and identifiable way; it is the flux of hungers and sentiments which assume particular forms chiefly in response to the flow of supplies. Because there is no demand for new and unknown goods, no demand for the unforeseeable fruits of innovation and genius, preoccupation with demand fosters stagnation. Egalitarianism in the economy tends to promote greed over giving. It downplays the various and specific sources of supply to favour the diffuse and sterile clamor for demand".

"French economist Jean-Baptiste Say, essentially maintained that the sum of wages, profits, and rents paid in manufacturing a good is sufficient to buy it. This does not mean that the same people who make a thing will buy it, but that they could. Therefore, across an entire system, purchasing power and producing power can always balance: there will always be enough wealth in an economy to buy its products".

"Supply creates its own demand may be a more felicitous way of putting it. But the essential point is fruitless to deny. Producers play a leading role in eliciting, shaping and creating demand. Investment decisions will be crucial in determining both the quantity and the essential pattern of consumer purchases".

"Capitalist creativity is guided not by any invisible hand, but by the quite visible and aggressive hand of management and entrepreneurship. Businesses continually differentiate their products, their marketing techniques, their advertising, and their retailing strategies in order to find some unique niche in the system from which they can reap, as long as possible, monopoly profits. Without the aid of Government, protecting patents or otherwise excluding competitors, these monopoly positions tend to be short-lived. But they are the goal of business strategy, the focus of creative entrepreneurship, the motivation of original research and development".

"Nonetheless, the crucial source of creativity and initiative in any economic system is the individual investor. Economies do not grow of their own accord or by dint of government influence. They grow in response to the enterprise of persons willing to take risks, to transform ideas into monopolies, and monopolies into industries, and to give before they know what they will get in return".

"This situation illuminates a central fallacy of demand-orientated economics. Demand orientated businesses rarely create new goods, for there is no measurable demand for what is not already familiar".

"What has happened is emergence of a final corollary of Say's law: subsidized supply destroys demand. Production without a willing market (e.g., infrastructure that is not needed) is a form of disguised consumption, and despite first appearances, it does not stimulate an economy. Nonproductive government spending, even when designed to spur demand, actually soon reduces it, regardless of any statistical increase in purchasing power. The artificial stimulus, like an addiction, requires even greater injections to sustain the initial effect.

When government gives welfare, unemployment payments and public-service jobs in quantities that deter productive work, and when it raises taxes on profitable enterprise to pay for them, demand declines. In fact, nearly all the programs that many economists advocate to promote equality and often rationalized in terms of stimulating consumption, in actuality reduce demand by undermining the production from which all real demand derives. Buying power does not essentially trickle down as wages or flow up and away as profits and savings. It originates with productive work at any level. This is the simple and homely first truth about wealth and poverty. Give, and you will be given unto. This is the secret not only of riches but also of growth.

This is also the essential insight of supply side economics. Governments cannot significantly affect real aggregate demand through policies of taxing and spending, taking money from one person and giving to another, whether in government or out. All this shifting of wealth is a zero sum game and the net effect on incomes is usual zero, or even negative".

Wealth and Poverty is an excellent publication well worth reading. For every creditor, there is a debtor. For every lender, there is a borrower. To blame the World Financial Crisis on a credit crunch seems simplistic to me. I believe Harry Dent's reasoning ("The Great Boom Ahead" 1993) makes more sense, a fundamental change in consumer spending due to age demographics. The credit squeeze could simply be a symptom.

Thinking analytically, it seems unlikely that a small credit problem in Asia could have caused a significant world economic downturn during the Asian Crisis (the currency devaluations and downturn that occurred in 1997). Also, a sub-prime mortgage problem seems unlikely to have manifested itself into the major worldwide downturn experienced during the later downturn. The reality may simply be that economic theory has not considered population demographics. Could this be why large economic cycles keep taking governments and economists by surprise? Could it be that our erstwhile economic gurus and leaders were so inside the picture? Is it possible these professors and financial leaders are unable to see another entire picture? Full credit to Harry Dent for thinking outside the box.

Incredibly Harry Dent also predicted that Australia would be relatively unaffected by the Sub-Prime economic downturn. He joked that he would emigrate to Australia before 2009. He attributed Australia's good fortune to two factors: Australia's population age demographics and the fact that Australia's main export market was an emerging Asia, including China. These predictions were made in a book published in 1999: *The roaring 2000's Investor*.

I believe that Mr Dent got it right and that the economic stimulus package has only distorted rather than assisted the economy. For example, the United States and Europe also introduced stimulus packages yet went through a significant downturn. Likewise, Japan has stagnated for more than decade despite regular attempts to stimulate its economy.

We all received a leaflet through the mail from the tax office titled *Business Tax break.* The leaflet explained the 30 and 50 per cent tax breaks being offered. New cars, vans, computers, and office furniture were included. Exempted were second-hand goods, capital works including most buildings, dams, trading stock, and software.

A prudent business that does not squander on new office furniture and motor vehicles but instead undergoes a capital project to expand production would not be eligible. That same business will pay more long-term tax to pay for the tax breaks (remember, it is all a zero-sum game), reducing its ability to expand. Yet logically, that capital project would stimulate the construction sector.

Let us not forget the simple truth that current production supports current living standards. On a macro scale, superannuation is not a store of the current output. The truth of this statement should have been brought home to people by the recent reduction in the value of their retirement schemes. Superannuation is not the answer to the world population age distribution problem.

We cannot live on credit indefinitely—not individuals, nor business entities, nor nations. When surplus countries such as China, Japan, OPEC nations, and India improve their living standards by increasing internal consumption, there will be downward pressure on living standards (consumption) in deficit nations as credit availability reduces. Thus, the time is overdue for first world nations to reject the flawed demand-side economic theory.

CHAPTER 3

PROTECTIONISM AND RISK

When businesses or individuals trade goods, they do so because it is mutually beneficial to each party. When nations trade with one another, they become better of because of that trade. Trade moves resources to where they are needed. Free trade benefits all countries, regardless of whether they are rich or poor. People working in the third world, producing goods for wealthy nations, are better off than before. When I was younger, mass starvation and famines were normal in India and China.

Tariffs and Duties prevent the efficient allocation of resources. Resources are transferred from more profitable industries to those that are less profitable. Australia needs to direct resources into the areas of its economy where the best returns are. Therefore, all tariffs, duties and other protections should be removed. Businesses need to compete on an equal footing. If we are going to protect industries in the third world (usually businesses that have reached their maturity stage), we should expect third world living standards. The price of labour is not an excuse for tariffs; we only want industries that can afford to pay the market rate for labour. Tariffs may protect wage rates in the protected industry but ultimately bring down average wage rates.

There needs to be a level playing field for Australia's industry. If legislation and local markets place costly requirements and expectations on Australian producers, then the same needs to be placed on imported goods where possible. We need to take into consideration the impact of labour 1 aws, quality assurance requirements, future emissions trading schemes (where polluters who want to increase their emissions must buy permits to pollute from others willing to sell them), and a host of other legislative requirements. Australian businesses that may otherwise be more efficient and profitable than their overseas competitors can be forced out of the market due to these additional burdens. We should remove unnecessary requirements, minimise the rest, and level the playing field with anti-dumping legislation (to counteract the damage done to local producers when foreign goods are overproduced due to subsidies, then the surplus exported to Australia at below market price).

Before WW2, Britain was one of the worlds least-regulated nations. From the mid-1700s onward, the industrial revolution began in Britain. Britain led the world in technology right through to WW2. Post-war, the British people, traumatized by the war, decided on new protectionism and a central planning model. Britain nationalized its rail system and other industries and protected a lot of its industry and labour force. In this environment, unionism flourished; the union movement (and governments of the day) resisted any restructuring that would result in temporary job losses. When technology frees up labour, then labour can be used more efficiently elsewhere. (The reason why a bulldozer driver has a higher income than a person in the undeveloped world, with a pick and shovel, is that he has replaced a hundred such people.) The UK economy stagnated. In the meantime, Japan, devastated by the war, invested heavily in new plant and equipment, and temporarily sacrificed living standards. This trend continued with the introduction of robotics on assembly lines.

Once the world's most industrialized nation, an uncompetitive Britain has now been relegated to the status of an average European economy. The UK's decline continues. To a certain extent, Britain's recent economy has been based on the financial sector and dot-com companies. This economy sector developed when Margaret Thatcher's government freed up the financial sector while it remained regulated elsewhere in Europe. I believe Britain's economy is in a perilous situation. Australia should not be emulating Britain's current regulated big government model as it is a failure.

Interestingly it is a fallacy that China's competitiveness is based solely on cheap labour. China can produce items like electric drills that retail for $30 in Australia because

China has also invested heavily in robotics. So the labour component of these products is minimal.

All economies are information economies where information can be substituted for other resources such as labour and raw materials (an example would be reduced fuel consumption due to telecommuting).

As information becomes cheaper, it is substituted for other inputs. This leads to cheaper goods, resulting in consumers with more discretionary spending money, leading to industrial development and wealth.

Any system designed to maintain the high cost of information by force, supporting producers at the expense of consumers, will come under stress. Personal computers and the internet shift the balance of power to consumers-people can receive, send, and produce information.

Customers can move the point of sale to ground more favourable to themselves. For example:

They use overseas stockbrokers (if fees are lower or tax laws more favourable).

Or they simply get people in countries where telecommunications are cheaper to ring back.

The sales revenue flows to the country where the point of sale originates. Value always flows to the least regulated, information finds its way around regulations, and services can be sold across borders via the internet to where those services may be regulated or illegal. The more regulated market loses the revenue. The internet is bringing about globalization.

If a government cannot accept the above implications, that government reduces that country to a follower, and opportunities go elsewhere.

The following is from an essay written by Frederic Bastiat (a member of the French parliament) in 1850.

"It is impossible to introduce into society a greater evil than this: the conversion of the law into an instrument of plunder. What are the consequences of such a perversion?

In the first place, it erases from everyone's conscience the distinction between justice and injustice.

Imagine that this fatal principle has been introduced: Under the pretence of organization, regulation, protection, or encouragement, the law takes property from one person and gives it to another; the law takes the wealth of all and gives it to a few—whether farmers, manufacturers, ship owners, artists, or comedians. Under these circumstances, then certainly every class will aspire to grasp the law, and logically so.

The excluded classes will furiously demand their right to vote—and will overthrow society rather than not to obtain it. Even beggars and vagabonds will then prove to you that they also have an incontestable title to vote. They will say to you, "we cannot buy wine, tobacco, or salt without paying the tax. And part of the tax we pay is given by law—in privileges and subsidies—to men who are richer than we are". Others use the law to raise the prices of bread, meat, iron, or cloth. Thus, since everyone else uses the law for his own profit, we also would like to use the law for our own profit. We demand from the law the right to relief, which is the poor man's plunder. To obtain this right, we also should be the voters and legislators in order that we may organize beggary on a grand scale for our class, as you have organized protection on a grand scale for your class.

The person who profits from this law will complain bitterly, defending his acquired rights. He will claim that the state is obligated to protect and encourage his particular industry; that this procedure enriches the state because the protected industry is thus able to spend more and to pay higher wages to the poor workingmen.

Do not listen to this sophistry by vested interests. The acceptance of these arguments will build legal plunder into a whole system. In fact, this has already occurred. The present day delusion is an attempt to enrich everyone at the expense of everyone else; to make plunder universal under the pretence of organizing it".

Well, the beggars and vagabonds now have the vote; however, Frederic Bastiat's underlying message is even more relevant today.

There is a relationship between market risk and return. When the average price/earnings ratio of a stock market becomes well above the long-term average, then that market is overvalued. When the ratio of "average house market value/average income" rises above the long-term average, the housing market is overvalued. Housing in Australia is currently overvalued (I do realise there are submarkets, but I am talking broadly), pushed up in price by the first-time homeowner grant and a belief that housing values always go up. The cause of the subprime crisis in the United States was that risk became separated (hidden) from return. Various financial securities became divorced from the housing assets they were invested in. That, along with the belief that Government would not leave people homeless, resulted in high risk-taking in the housing market.

The market needs information. Investors need to know the level of risk they are taking on when making investment decisions. Thus, the sub-prime market crisis is not a failure of the market (as many would suggest) but rather a consequence of lack of information flowing to investors combined with a tendency for the government to overprotect the housing market (i.e., a failure of government).

Protecting people from risk and from the consequences of their actions, leads to overheated markets. It seems strange that a rock climber may legally climb without the aid of ropes, whereas an individual constructing a structure for his use must wear a safety harness above a certain height. Apparently, under present workplace standards regulations, it is all right to take risks in pursuing leisure, but not all right if trying to do something constructive. I believe employers have a duty of care towards their employees;

however, personal empowerment and responsibilities should be considered for personal risk-taking. We cannot legislate to make everyone one hundred per cent safe. It would have been illegal for the Wright brothers (I believe that Richard Pierce made an earlier flight) to risk that first flight. No risk-taking means stagnation. Most of the world light aircraft were built in the 1970s and earlier. American companies such as Cessna no longer construct them due to fear of litigation and high insurance premiums. Consequently, an attempt to make companies accountable for safety has resulted in the world relying on forty-year-old aircraft for its light aircraft fleet.

Risk-taking is a part of progress. New entrepreneurs must risk everything in the expectation of an eventual return. Current safety regulations are reaching a level where they are absurd. You should not protect people from the consequences of their actions (personal responsibility).

The following principle is so basic it should not need stating, but many are in denial. An iron law of economics is that labour is a commodity and an expense. If expenses such as labour rise, net profit declines for affected businesses. Some businesses may close while others curtail expansion plans. Artificially high wages reduce employment opportunities. Artificially high wages in large-scale manufacturing, pushed up as a consequence of industrial action, reduces that industry's ability to expand.

Inflexible employment laws, likewise, impose a cost on business. The recently repealed work choices legislation could not reduce the underlying average wage; underlying average wages, like any other commodity, are determined by supply and demand, (i.e., the strength of the economy). Any business that drops wages too low will simply lose its best staff to other businesses. This is an unalterable cast-iron fact, just like the laws of physics are unalterable.

Workers should have a right to representation when signing a contract. Industrial Law needs to consider the clad in iron unalterable laws of economics. It has become politically incorrect to state the facts. However, it is not union-bashing to state an iron-clad unalterable law.

Finally, I would like to mention protectionism and responsibility as it relates to government itself. If a private sector business makes a poor decision, it places its profit at risk. The businesspeople concerned may lose their income and even their assets. If an individual in the state sector makes a poor decision, that person rarely loses income or personal assets. Often there is no individual accountability; the individual can hide in the system, mistakes made costing the taxpayer or ratepayer instead.

If an individual or entity in the private sector is successfully sued over a public liability issue, then that individual or entity pays. If the state is successfully sued, those who made the flawed decision do not pay; the taxpayer or ratepayer does.

Within the state sector, there is no urgency; in the private sector, time is money. In the state sector, following procedure and avoiding personal responsibility is the order of the day. When the state sector and private sector interact, it is like two alien worlds meeting.

CHAPTER 4

DECENTRALISATION, FREE SPEECH, AND SELF-ESTEEM

Who would have thought more than 30 years ago that a concept called the internet would put a large portion of all knowledge at a person's fingertips? The power of the internet is described in the book *Future Wealth:* **Investing in the Second Great wave of Technology** by Francis McInerney and Sean White (St Martin's Press 2000), which is well worth reading. It says, "Our ability to substitute information at will for every other resource is. The falling cost of information improves productivity, keeps inflation low, and drives sales".

The internet increases consumer power. It allows consumers to bypass intermediaries and go straight to producers. It makes it easier for consumers to shop around.

The Australian government is spending a substantial sum on fibre optics for fast internet (Elon Musk's Starlink system may change the necessity). There will be a faster payback on the project if some of the restrictions preventing the bypassing of middlemen are removed. Internet auction sites would bring buyers and sellers together. In the case of land sales only, there should be no contract till a written contract is signed (i.e., the internet simply brings the two parties together (for personal protection). Such websites should also display a warning that purchasers should consult a lawyer before signing anything.

However, valuers and estate agents should not be protected industries. For example, I cannot see any reason for sale price information being restricted to these industries. Does it matter if your neighbour has access to how much you paid for your house? You should be able to shop around online for the property of your dreams and not be hoodwinked by estate agents as to its value. If you can do your own searching, you are more likely to make the right decision instead of being led by an estate agent. One reason estate agents charge such high fees is that they need to, as they make few sales, partly because there are too many in the industry. (Everyone wants to be an estate agent.) The internet has the power to bypass the whole industry. The same applies to all selling, such as purchasing motor vehicles.

Fast internet combined with the freedom of information (I stress 'freedom of information') will be a powerful tool for economic growth. The time will come when television and the internet will be one. Fast real-time internet means anyone can set up a mini-TV station with a simple digital camera. Viewers will have a choice of thousands of channels. Existing broadcasters that have invested heavily in infrastructure will find that it has been devalued. I have been disappointed by the lack of in-depth analysis reporting by current media. Media reporting is ratings-driven. Reporting tends to be superficial and sensationalist.

I do understand that it is a marketing tool. The revenue comes from ads, and everything in between is simply a filler to keep us viewing. The media is ratings-driven, as this dictates the advertising revenue that can be obtained. I am disappointed, as the potential was for TV to be a powerful marketing tool. Instead, reporting has become superficial, and programming seems to be largely composed of violent American 'cops and robbers' rubbish.

Another issue is censorship by technology companies. The main social media platforms have become monopolies. Anyone using a smaller competitor simply does not have a big enough audience, so smaller social media platforms cannot get traction. In a democracy, freedom of speech is so important. If someone censors, that person's view of what is acceptable may differ from yours. The person's political views can influence the decision to sensor. Let the public have free access to all information and trust people to formulate their views. The argument is that a private company has the right to decide who uses its platform. My counterargument is that the argument is only valid if adequate competition exists. Therefore, legislation should ensure that these platforms do not include sensors (unless a person is promoting lawbreaking).

At election time, it would make sense for politicians to have uninterrupted opportunities to place before and explain to the public their economic policies and the logic behind them. Instead, we have this election debate nonsense where politicians over-talk one another, have no time to explain issues, and are constantly interrupted by biased interviewers. It is simply a form of entertainment; the public learns little from it. Yet, in a democracy, it is so important for the voter to be informed and make well-informed decisions.

Nonsense terms like right-wing and left-wing, socialist and capitalist, simply confuse the real issues and should be avoided. The real issue is central control and planning versus decentralization and handing power back to individuals and society.

Central planning and control have in the past given us the worst of government. Hitler's National Socialist Germany and Stalin's Soviet Union were examples of central planning and control. Both regimes were almost identical, yet one is labelled right-wing and the other left-wing. Almost everyone is a socialist in that liberals, conservatives, and Labour Party supporters all believe in a social safety net and achieving social outcomes. On the other hand, everyone is a capitalist: you are a capitalist if you own something and have a bank account. Using labels only creates confusion (often intentionally).

We must challenge political correctness as it stifles open to debate. For example, it is no longer politically correct to challenge climate change theory. Such people are labelled as planet wreckers, yet open debate on this issue is so important. When it becomes politically incorrect to debate certain topics, the discussion is channelled down a pathway. The issue is—who decides what is incorrect?

The following is an example of news reporting I listened to on Australian Television. "There has been an increase in thyroid cancer in children around Fukushima".

Fact—Japan put in place an extremely rigorous thyroid cancer testing program in the area. The increase in cancer detected was simply because it was being found earlier. The same result would have happened globally if the same testing program had been implemented (ref: www. hiroshimasyndrome.com/fukushima-child-thyroid-issue. html). The statement made has never been rebutted.

In the interests of appearing unbiased, the media interview people who claim to be experts but often ignore those employed or qualified in the subject (a biased style of interview). All sorts of unsupported statements are made in these interviews. Often complex answers are required, but a confrontational, interruption-filled interview style does not allow for this.

Trial by media, when the subject cannot speak out for fear comments may be prejudicial to a court case, is a disgrace. Media can influence a subsequent jury.

I agree that the media needs to be independent. The freedom of information and speech is an important part of democracy. I would like to see a private business sector television channel get an alternative view to the current news reporting that seems to me to be ratings-driven and biased. Knowledge is important in a democracy. At election time, politicians from all parties should give speeches on public media without reporter interruptions. The media can comment afterwards, but at least let the person get their point across.

To me (not a sports follower), there appears to be a disproportionate amount of sports reporting. This is fine if it is what the public want. My brother always used to say, "Football is a plot to keep the masses subdued". I say this tongue in cheek. (I am not actually anti-sports reporting, just making a point re: priorities.)

It takes self-esteem to speak contrary to prevailing views. Personal empowerment fosters self-esteem. People should fight against political correctness and should have enough self-esteem to be an individual rather than part of the mass. Don't be like Hitler's masses, who went along for the ride due to, in their case, the justified fear of being individuals. People should not fear censure for expressing a view (except in extreme cases promoting the infringement of the rights of others, such as promoting racism). All ideas are good ideas. The idea itself should be analysed-never attack the individual. This is a principle parliamentarians need to adhere to. I suspect the strategy politicians have of attacking their colleagues is in part due to a reluctance of the media to report the mundane.

The following is a quote from a communication and leadership program I once attended.

"You could learn that you can't be loved by everyone. You may be the finest plum in the world: ripe, juicy, and succulent—and offer yourself to all …and there will be some people who do not like plums. You must understand that if you are the world's finest plum, and someone you like doesn't happen to like plums, you have a choice of becoming a banana. And you must be warned that if you choose to become a banana, you will be a second-rate banana.

And you can always be the best plum. You must also realise, if you choose be a second-rate banana, there will be some people who do not like bananas. Furthermore, you could spend your life attempting to become the best banana, which is impossible if you are a plum, *or* you can seek again to be the best plum."

Your hurts come not from what others do to you; they come from what you choose to do with your actions.

The principles of personal empowerment and responsibility apply to the workplace. Some years ago, a phenomenon called "High-Performance Work Teams within the industry" swept through the United States. This concept has since spread throughout the world. The old top-down hieratical approach was replaced in many companies, and the whole structure flattened out, resulting in the disappearance of middle management as we know it. The ground floor workforce was organized into teams, who, on a consensus basis, were empowered with making decisions about their workplace, decisions that were once made by management. Once given the responsibility and control over their jobs, self-esteem, pride, etc., flourished. A happy workforce in these restructured companies began putting forward and adopting entrepreneurial new ideas. They are more closely in contact with the job (management were a few steps removed), and many heads are better than one (I am not saying that because I lived in Tasmania) provided people respect one another.

Contrast this with many areas of government. In many places, there are unnecessary layers of hierarchy. In other areas, sections are not actually needed (in New Zealand in the mid-1980's many quangos- quasi-autonomous government organisations were found to be unnecessary). Then there is petty cost-cutting. Imagine doing a job that is not needed and having to gain approval for any decisions constantly. What does this do for self-esteem? Welcome to the world of government.

Handing power back to individuals and entities fosters self-esteem, pride, and innovation. This principle applies to organizations (high-performance work teams) and society (e.g., getting big brother—government—out of people's lives).

Splitting up monopolies is also a way of decentralizing companies and handing power (consumer choice) back to individuals.

Empathy is sensing another's feelings and attitudes. Creating empathy involves taking others' concerns seriously and listening actively, encouraging further elaboration and clarification, reserving judgment and blame, displaying interest in what others communicate, and supporting others' attempts to find a solution. Contrast this with the aggressive approach between parliamentary members of different parties. Changing your mind and admitting mistakes is a part of learning, yet the reality of party politics is that politicians rarely do this.

We need to be a society of strong independent individuals, not brain-dead conformists who look to the government for every solution. The reality is that the government does not have the answers; we need the ability to take control of our lives and find solutions to our dilemmas to achieve individual goals.

Finally, maturity is learning to understand and control an emotion we all share: envy. It has led to the persecution of the well-off communist revolutions, Jews in Germany, and Indian shopkeepers in Uganda. Envy of success is an emotion central planners and controllers use to gain the support of the masses.

CHAPTER 5

SMALL GOVERNMENT AND TAX

Federalism was a structure created by the six British colonies in Australia. The British Parliament enacted legislation to allow the colonies to be federated in 1901. Originally separate colonies were established due to distance. Modern communications and transport have negated this problem. Nations with a much larger population than Australia (such as the UK) do not have a federal system. Federalism is simply a duplication of government services and imposes a large cost on Australians. Australia does not need separate state governments. Each state does not require different road rules, regulations, industrial relations laws, etc. We even have separate state police forces. Decentralisation and reducing the size of government is not about handing power to state governments; it is about handing power to individuals and private sector entities.

Till recently, I owned a greenhouse, and it became obvious to me recently just how dumb the system is. Some chemicals, registered as safe throughout Australia, are not available to Tasmanian growers. This is simply because separate registration is required in Tasmania. As the Tasmanian industry is small, it is not worth the cost of repeating the registration process. This sort of duplication is simply a waste of resources. In certain situations where particular circumstances apply to a particular state, this can still be catered for by a nationwide government. Often, state governments are at odds with the federal government, preventing genuine reform. A good example was when the state governments failed to remove stamp duties and land taxes when GST was introduced.

The Senate does not represent the population of Australia on a proportional basis. Tasmania has a half million citizens and twelve senators, New South Wales, eight million people and twelve senators. This senate then blocks legislation previously passed by the more representative house of representatives, often creating inertia. The smaller states may resist any change to their status.

Quotes from Australia's Constitution:

P. 10: "This Act, and all the laws made by the Parliament of the Commonwealth under the Constitution shall be binding on the courts, Judges, and the people of every state and of every part of the Commonwealth, not withstanding anything in the laws of any State; and the laws of the Commonwealth shall be in force on all British Ships, the Queen's ships of war excepted, whose first port of clearance and whose port of destination are in the commonwealth".

Does this mean British warships can do as they please in Australia's waters?

P. 11: "The States shall mean such of the colonies of New South Wales, New Zealand, Queensland, Tasmania, Victoria, Western Australia, and South Australia, including the Northern Territory of South Australia, as for the time being are parts of the Commonwealth".

New Zealand? (In my view, it would be great if it were a part of Australia.)

P. 22: "For the purposes of the last section, if by the law of any state all persons of any race are disqualified from voting at elections for the more numerous House of the Parliament of the State, then, in the reckoning the number of the people of the State or of the Commonwealth, persons of that race resident in that state shall not be counted."

I propose that Australians get rid of the state governments. As it is a constitutional matter, it could only be achieved through a referendum. Federalism is a shambles imposed on Australia more than one hundred years ago by Britain. I believe it would be very difficult to bring change about. (It can only be done via referendum.) Still, I also think it will be important for Australia's future prosperity and well-being.

As for Republicanism, I would prefer staying in the commonwealth as I am fond of tradition, even though I recognize that the monarchy is an archaic system based on privilege, however, it is a non-issue. This issue makes no difference to Australia's future. Australia is self-governing. Other nations will not behave differently towards Australia. So let us focus on the critical points.

Many industries use complex operations research techniques to determine limiting factors in production. The industry knows that when marginal variable costs exceed marginal returns, then production should be curtailed. The government, however, does not even apply a basic cost of compliance to society test to new legislation. I also propose that a new piece of legislation be introduced. This legislation will require that all new bills and regulations go through a benefit to society versus a cost of compliance to society test. The most recent legislation recently enacted would probably not pass this test. Little thought has been given to the additional costs being placed on the private sector. The government has been fighting fires with more and more regulations, and little thought has been given to the cost to society of trying to comply with it all.

Dumping the Privy Council as the final court of appeal was, in my opinion, a mistake. The Privy Council could not override Australian legislation. What it did do was place interpretations made by Australian Judges under scrutiny from leading UK (and Canadian) judges. It is good to have outside scrutiny. Having an international final appeal court also means that international entities will not question the impartiality of decisions. A final court of appeals consisting of Judges from like-minded countries (Canada and the UK) and Australian judges is a good idea. Maybe Australia should discuss the issue with these nations.

Dr Patrick Caragata (former New Zealand Inland Revenue Department chief policy advisor), working with a team of economists was employed by the Inland Revenue Department to study the impact of taxation. The study came to an interesting conclusion concerning taxation. They theorized that there is an optimum tax rate (common sense, really). If taxes are below the optimum, increasing taxes increases government revenue. However, if the tax rate is above that optimum, increasing taxes reduces government revenue. The Caragata study concluded that cutting tax (for New Zealand by one per cent would result in more than one per cent economic growth. The study also concluded that the growth maximizing rate would be between 16 and 25 per cent. The reasons are as follows:

- New businesses will prefer a lower tax environment overseas if rates are high.
- Investors will follow their money overseas.
- Entrepreneurs have less to reinvest into their businesses.
- High taxes result in less consumption expenditure.

The Caragata study assessed New Zealand's tax rate as being well above the optimum. The Caragata study also concluded that reducing taxes by one per cent would increase our growth rate by more than one per cent. The report was ignored. Incredibly, Australia has never done a similar study. It is common sense that increasing taxes above a certain level will suppress the private sector and reduce the tax base.

People have voted for high taxes to get more health and education funding. The reality is that higher taxes can, and have, reduced the tax base leaving even less for these services.

The post-WW2 period until now will be remembered as the era of big government. The following statistics apply to New Zealand, although Australia will have similar results:

In the 1920s, the government took 12 per cent of GDP in taxes. In the 1930s, the percentage had increased to 16. In the 1940s through till the 1960s, the tax take was 25 per cent. It was 27 per cent in the 1970s. In the 1980s it increased to 31 per cent. In the 1990s it rose to 35 per cent. This has been the trend throughout the Western World. Is there any surprise that our economies are stagnant?

Income tax has become excessively complex, requiring an army of accountants to bookkeep for individuals and businesses. We have various exemptions and a graduated tax scale because governments have confused the roles of revenue gathering and social security—an army of tax and estate planners arranging individuals and business affairs to minimize their tax burden. The compliance costs of tax accounting (including withholding employee tax) are high for small businesses (for New Zealand 2.4 per cent of GDP; *Closing the Gaps*, ACT NZ Parliamentary Office, 2001, 40).

Income tax is not a level playing field. An example: why should an employee not claim travel getting to work and other expenses associated with his work when a person doing the same job, but as a contractor, can? Under the tax rules, different industries are treated differently because of political interference. Prime agricultural land, for example, may not be used for the highest and best use due to tax concessions for forestry. Our tax legislation has evolved in a hodgepodge manner over a long period to satisfy the whims of various politicians. Incredible as it sounds, the whole lot needs to be dumped for a simple broad-based system that creates a level playing field.

In his book Unfinished Business, Sir Roger Douglas (who has received the prestigious Swedish Hayek medal for services to economics), a former finance minister of New Zealand, proposed completely replacing income tax. Introducing compulsory health insurance (subsidized for low-income people) accounts for education (reduced as income levels rise). Efficient small government, then a small GST increase, plus making GST exemption complimentary, would enable the complete removal of income tax and other distorting taxes such as stamp duties, gift and death duties, land tax and tariffs, etc. Income reporting would still need to be a requirement to allow for social security assistance. GST should have been an exemption-free broad-based replacement tax, not an additional tax. GST is a tax on consumption rather than production; it changes the emphasis. Income tax has passed its use-by date and can be leapfrogged by GST. Income reporting would still be needed; subsidizing education and health for low-income people helps compensate for

GST is not a graduated tax. However, things need to be as transparent and straightforward as possible; we do not want another estate planning industry developing to maximize subsidies.

I believe that a universal basic income scheme should be considered. This concept has been around a while now and is a payment made to all adult citizens irrespective of their income. Complexity should be engineered out of our society; a universal minimum income scheme would even negate people's need to report income, as the same payment is made to everyone. The less complex structures are, the more efficient society is. Reduced administration leads to more efficient use of resources and economic growth. One big criticism is that it would be difficult to decide who would go onto the mentoring program (described in chapter six). A universal basic income scheme is a flat payment incentivizing self-advancement. Another criticism is the need for a high tax rate to enable the concept. Basic income schemes also come under criticism because they do not generate government revenue (which is not their purpose); what is distributed equates to the additional revenue gathered. The sole purpose of such a scheme is a simplified redistribution process. The payment rate should be set at a level that enables people to live without poverty but still creates an incentive for self-advancement. (Unfortunately, deciding what poverty is is subjective.) Yet another criticism is that the well-off also get the same payment. This criticism derives from a lack of understanding. The well off contributes more than they get back—Vis-versa for the less well off. The scheme is so structured for simplification. Because this wage is derived from GST receipts, the net effect is redistribution. I have explained why redistribution is a zero-sum game as far as promoting economic growth. However, I have neglected one aspect, a large wealth gap, and being inhumane, also reduces the ability of those adversely impacted to reach their full potential. A simple payment to all in society minimizes any economic impact that would be caused by inequitable distribution. Although I have no doubt some will bemoan that the well-off also get the payment, it could be difficult to explain the logic of simplification to many.

Replacing income tax negates the need for much of an entire estate planning industry and so much more. A universal basic income considerably reduces the role of the government welfare agency Centrelink. These are examples of what I mean by engineering out complexity. Governments tend to tinker with what already exists when instead they should be asking, is there a better, simple way?

Finally, about tax, I believe that the government should not be placing itself above individual citizens as if it has some exalted status. Government is there to serve us—by the people, of the people, for the people. For this reason, when the tax liability is in dispute, the burden of proof should be with the tax department. If a private sector service provider has a dispute with a debtor, they need to take that debtor to court and prove liability.

The government is a glorified service provider with more resources than individuals. In liability cases involving the tax office, the same rules should apply. Also, in bankruptcy cases, small subcontractors, often good viable businesses, can be put at risk due to moneys owed by a firm going into bankruptcy. The tax office places itself ahead of unsecured creditors when the residue is being dished out. In the case of bankruptcies, I believe the tax office should payout GST owed on outstanding expenses but line upon an equal footing with unsecured creditors for GST receipts on current sales. These changes would be a first step in recognizing that the state exists for its citizens; citizens are not here for the state.

Local bodies need to focus on a user pays for services approach. Rates based upon land values are an anachronism. Worse still are rates based upon the capital value, which bears no relationship to services provided (in fact, the value of your car probably bears more of a relationship). The assumption is that people who live in more expensive accommodation or own farms are somehow better off financially. The reality is that a person's financial position often bears little relationship to property values. Also, there appears to be a disproportionate amount of rates being paid by rural areas. Councils should not be making income redistribution decisions. These are best left to Centrelink, which has better information on the financial position of those in need.

Another problem is in areas that are in decline. Local body revenue does not drop in response as there is an ongoing rating on vacant residential and commercial buildings. This can result in more lavish spending on capital projects than the population in these areas may warrant.

Councils are locally elected and represent local issues. This is a good concept, but there are many concerns. Voters invariably know little about those they are electing. Perhaps there should be a list on the council internet site. This could list all issues voted on during council meetings and the way each councillor voted. Electors need information. Local councils pass a lot of silly by-laws and regulations. Maybe an independent body could again apply a cost to society test on by-laws. (The issue I would have is that yet another organisation, at a price, is being created?) I take exception to the fact that town planners can sometimes use insider information (I am sure it happens). Maybe information should be publicly available at the early planning stages? Markets need information. There should be closer monitoring and good penalties to stamp out insider opportunism.

A system that more closely links services provided (by local bodies) to the users of those services, rather than a land-based system, would result in service users making judgements like, do we need this service, given what it costs us? There is one acceptable argument for land value rates. High rates on high-value land ensure that this land is utilized, part of ensuring land is used for its highest and best use. However, I believe the emphasis should be on user pays.

Business people must be ethical to remain in business. There are exceptions, but usually, word gets around fast. Rather than taking and consuming, entrepreneurs give and risk. Selling equates to giving for an expectation of a matching gift in anticipation of return. The entrepreneur does not expect anything for anything. The entrepreneur risks everything when creating his skills. Trust is an essential part of entrepreneurship. An entrepreneur cannot succeed unless his product appeals to the wants and needs of others.

The state sector, by its nature, does not have the same generous approach of only receiving by giving something of equal value. The state sector takes from the private sector and spends (consumes). It is a spending culture. Often, this spending is not on what is wanted and needed by society; it is at the whim of politicians and bureaucrats. They are outside the control of the market; it is a take-by-force and spends culture.

Those wealth creators who have part of the proceeds of their efforts redistributed should expect a degree of accountability and responsibility from the recipients.

CHAPTER 6

SOCIAL STRUCTURE, HEALTH, EDUCATION, AND LAW AND ORDER SOCIAL STRUCTURE

Imagine a young male, a child in a single-parent household. His mother is concerned about his welfare. However, she also has numerous boyfriends but has no long-term relationship (she can't put her Centrelink payments at risk).

The young person could be abused, suffer neglect, etc. He then mixes with a poor peer group, suffers substandard education, and, ultimately, his girlfriend may become pregnant. Like most males, he feels protective towards her and wishes to remain in a relationship with her. (Obviously, I've written this from a male perspective.) However, she no longer has a use for him; she is better off financially without him due to her Centrelink entitlements.

Result: one uneducated alienated, angry young male with no sense of purpose and a **danger** to society.

Issues –

- Poorly thought-out payments giving wrong incentives;
- Child's parents unable to remove the child from bad peer pressure (school choice would help enable this);
- Sole custody means one natural parent has little input into the child's well-being; and
- Sole custody removes one parent's sense of purpose and responsibility.

Our social system lacks two fundamental ingredients: personal empowerment and personal responsibility.

Personal empowerment – giving people the ability to make decisions for themselves.

Examples of elements of personal empowerment:

- A mentor system so that young people can have a person alongside them to teach and advise on life skills and to act as a role model.
- Giving people control over decisions, such as which school to send their children to.

There is nothing more satisfying than having control over your life, setting goals, and achieving them.

Personal responsibility–people are accepting responsibility for the decisions they make.

Don't reward people for making the wrong decisions. If a person is constantly told he is stupid, he will play out due to lower self-esteem. Excessive regulation is, in effect, telling people that they are stupid.

Having a social safety net is essential. However, simply handing money over without any accountability is creating both a cargo-cult mentality. (After World War two, certain Pacific Islands began to receive aid. Many Islanders stopped harvesting food the traditional way and instead would wait for the next cargo ship.) and a system open to abuse. We need trained people who can act as mentors and look at what is happening in these families. We need to produce well-adjusted people with values, accept responsibility for their actions, and prepare to take risks, make good decisions, and recognize that making mistakes is part of the learning process. If the principles of personal empowerment and responsibility are considered before any government decision-making, we as individuals will respond.

I appreciate that the example given is extreme and represents only a tiny percentage of cases. I also recognize that many young people lack the necessary maturity to accept responsibility. They simply do not think about the consequences of their actions and are not motivated by baby bonuses and centre link payments. I also respect the fact that many solo parents are good parents. However, none of this negates the fact that social security should be based on personal responsibility and empowerment, including adequate mentoring.

It is cruel to leave people in a welfare comfort zone without goals and participation in society. There needs to be a stick-and-carrot approach to social security. Options include time limits on dole payments. Once the time limit expires, a ticket system (no cash in hand) could kick in (such a system would probably be impractical if a universal basic income scheme is in place but is still worth debating). Maybe social payments could be lower in areas with little prospect of finding work; people encouraged to relocate with relocation costs covered?

Mentoring

I believe a significant reason for the social breakdown in our society is the breakdown of the family unit. At one time, the elderly, middle-aged and young lived together as one family unit. The elderly had a lifetime of experience and would mentor the young. Today, often, the young are isolated and left to seek solutions alone. The elderly often live alone and are no longer valued.

Mentors could assess a person's actual needs rather than simply handing over the money with no accountability. We have a whole army of retired people who have a lifetime of experience and could volunteer as mentors (with some form of remuneration, perhaps a pension top-up for doing voluntary community work?). Training would be involved, and such mentors should not be placed in dangerous situations. I am not sure how it will be decided who goes onto a mentoring program if a universal basic income scheme, as described earlier, is introduced. This is something that should be debated.

My lovely late wife Kaye (who dedicated her life to helping young people) was a see-you-at-home nurse. This is a voluntary program for teenage pregnant girls. The program teaches parenting skills, skills such as child nutrition, interacting with their child, child health and general parenting skills. Good nutrition has an impact on brain development. Suppose a parent interacts with and is responsive to their child's needs, then there is a greater likelihood of that child becoming a well-adjusted adult. This type of program passes the latest research from academics to right where it needs to be.

A problem we have is that modern television promotes the extremes as normality. Most people lead a relatively moral-ethical life. However, we are fed a diet of soapies that promote the concept of people sleeping around and moving from one relationship to another as normal. People are no longer sitting around the family meal table discussing issues but instead are glued to this nonsense; my concern is that social values are being chipped away.

Many young people with low expectations have poor communication skills. They are full of bravado, critical and respond to criticism with aggression rather than a reasoned response. These teenagers have a small-town mentality; they cannot see an ambitious future. This can be an intergenerational problem, which is why outside mentoring is so significant.

An economy is the decisions made by its people, their skills, how they interact, their expectations. An economy is its people and is for its people. An economy is of the people for the people.

Shared Parenting

I support the new shared parenting legislation. No system is perfect; problems include the need for young babies to have consistency, to bond (you cannot share parent babies) and the need for frequent commuting between households.

However, "Children in joint physical custody arrangements were found to have better adjustment on depression, deviance, school effort and school grades than those in sole custody" (Buchanan, Maccoby and Dornbusch, Harvard University Press 1996).

The March 2002 issue of "Journal of Family Psychology" published by the American Psychological Assoc. States that children in Joint custody settings have fewer behavioural and emotional problems have higher self-esteem, better family relations and better school performance.

For those who still do not believe that shared parenting is the best arrangement, rather than sole custody, I refer you to a Canadian website – www.glen-net.ca. It states that 85 per cent of all rapists are motivated by displacement anger; 71per cent of high school dropouts and 85 per cent of all youth in prison come from fatherless homes.

Raising the next generation is the most important thing parents can do. A stable environment is so important. Providing a stable family unit and the willingness of parents to place their children's needs ahead of their own is what is needed. If young women need to be motivated by a baby bonus, they may not be in a stable relationship or a sound financial situation. The baby bonus should be dumped.

Crime

Crime was considered quite literally to be out of control in New York in the early eighties. The city was considered to be a dangerous place to visit. A new program was instigated, zero tolerance to crime. This simply involved robust policing and tougher penalties for petty crime. Police rigorously pursued petty crimes such as graffiti. The logic was, firstly, that petty criminals often eventually become serious hardened offenders. Secondly, it was reasoned that serious offenders also commit petty crimes.

We have youth laws, which mean young offenders are untouchable and do not suffer consequences until they become hardened criminals. Stricter youth laws, ensuring young offenders suffer the consequences of their actions, reduces the likelihood of their moving on to more serious crimes.

The New York solution was as simple as described above, yet the city's crime rate steadily fell and is only a fraction of its 1980s level.

Most violent offenders re-offend within three years of release. They are vacating their cells for a short time to create more mayhem and harm more victims. The politically correct government has decided that we can reform violent offenders by being nice to them. It hasn't worked. We have allowed a prison culture to flourish in our prisons, where the evilest, violent prisoners often dominate and are role models for other prisoners.

Some time ago, I watched a documentary about a privately run prison in the US. An ex-prisoner was running this prison. The guards constantly watched over them, the intention being to prevent a prison culture from developing. Here, any inmate attempting to dominate or not show respect for another had his privileges removed and was often isolated. Inmates attended various programs related to social skills and were quite literally expected to ask for permission to go to the toilet. Guards did not like working in this prison because it was hard work. However, there was little re-offending upon release.

Health

I recently watched a documentary comparing different health system models. The conclusion was that the US system, a mix of state and private, was a shambles. The British National Health System was no better. Only one nation stood out, that nation being Japan. In Japan, waiting lists were almost non-existent, and everyone had easily accessible access to healthcare.

In Japan, everyone has health insurance. The entire health system is in the private sector. However, the government regulates the cost of pharmaceuticals and doctors' fees.

So, if this model has proven to be so successful, why not emulate it? People will be empowered in that they will be able to choose their own insurance company and hospital. Insurance fees could be subsidized for low-income people. A competitive private-sector health model is the answer to eliminating all the bureaucracy and wastage in the present system.

A system of mentoring for welfare recipients is a step towards preventative health. Lifestyle choices cannot be imposed on people, but education and mentoring are steps in the right direction. Even small things like doctors automatically giving patients a copy of their health records would help patients monitor their progress.

Overeating, poor diet, a sedentary lifestyle, smoking, and to a lesser extent, road accidents and other accidents are among the biggest drains on the health system. Early man evolved as a hunter-gatherer and travelled (and ran) long distances in an environment where food was scarce and obtaining it was hard work. As a result, our bodies do cope well but simply are not designed to handle a sedentary lifestyle and overeating.

Research worldwide shows a correlation between health and such things as income, qualifications, and status. Our habits are influenced by our families, our friends, and our workmates. An individual's social setting is a major factor. A person's environment is another factor; if you work long hours as a taxi driver, it is hard to get those thirty minutes of vigorous daily exercise that you need.

The psychology of humans is complex. Placing pressure on people to change their habits can have the counterproductive effect of making people feel unworthy. Low self-esteem results in lethargy. I believe these issues need to be understood if we are to have an effective preventative health program.

It is annoying when the media tells us that low-income people have a poor diet because they are on a small budget. The reality is that healthy food (usually unprocessed food) costs less; you can buy a bag of spuds for the cost of a bag of potato chips. The issues are more complex.

Obesity and its associated health issues are a major problem for Australia. I have recently found out that the priority given for treatment in hospitals in Australia is based on quality altered life years. An insurance premium scheme could also prioritize healthcare decisions if set up correctly. Such a scheme will send a strong message to those leading an unhealthy lifestyle (e.g., smoking and alcohol) when that lifestyle affects their pocket (results in higher premiums).

Education

Give parents control over decisions, such as which school to send their children to. Regardless of social background, parents wish nothing but the best for their children. There is nothing more satisfying than having control over your life.

Education Accounts is a concept that has come out of the poorer areas of the United States. It involves allocating an education account to each school-age child, with a sum of money in it that approximately equates to the cost of educating that child. Parents send their children to the school they perceive as likely to achieve the best results (if space is available and regardless of whether the school is public or private). The school can then draw its fees from the account. This should result in the highest achieving schools getting the most extensive roles and competition between schools, a plus for education. (It is a good result if under-performing schools do not get adequate enrollments, who wants substandard schools?) This is a decentralized model with the central government having no say in the school's decisions, provided a basic curriculum and code of conduct is followed. There should continue to be a national external exam system so that the calibre of teachers and schools can be assessed, and that assessment should be available to parents.

The above structure should result in good teachers becoming a sought-after commodity who are well remunerated. If they are not, schools will lose them. Also, spending will become better targeted towards results. For example, is a computer for every child a way of getting the best outcome? I have heard some educationists say that tossing every computer out of schools would improve learning outcomes as young children are not thinking when tapping a keyboard. For me, the computer for every child campaign is reminiscent of a Soviet Grand central plan. Instead, decentralize and let schools make the spending decisions. In a competitive environment, they will work out the best way of achieving results. I would like to refer readers to Deborah Coddington's book *Let Parents Choose* (Valentine Press). This excellent publication goes into more detail and gives further references on the subject.

There also needs to be more emphasis on early childhood education, parents acting as teachers, and it is important to get books into homes. Mentors can help emphasise the importance of (and give advice regarding) early childhood education to parents.

Truancy can be a significant problem. In the United States, Jacksonville High School had a challenging but successful way of dealing with the situation. If a truancy officer picked up truant children, that child's parents would be contacted. The parents were required to sign a contract stating how they would get their children to school in the future. Noncompliance could result in one or more of the parents being incarcerated. The Florida Tims-Union (Jacksonville. com) 22 Oct. 2014 states When an arrest warrant is filed, the parents have been offered help and counselling at the school level, then referred to the state attorneys office's arbitration team. An arrest is the last resort. Parents can be charged with contributing to the delinquency of a minor and can face up to a year in jail.

CHAPTER 7

GLOBAL WARMING

The first thing I would like to say about Global Warming is to make sure we have our facts right. It's not a good thing to continuously pump more carbon dioxide into the atmosphere. However, we do need a rational debate on the matter. Anyone who disputes the calamitous global warming scenario is largely ignored, accused of having their head in the sand and labelled as a planet wrecker. All ideas are good ideas.

The ratio of atmospheric carbon dioxide to oxygen has remained in equilibrium for hundreds of millions of years, although the ratio has been falling up until the industrial age. It is now understood that the oxygenation of the atmosphere was caused by photosynthesis within microbes over a billion years or more. (Simple cells have been around for 3.5 billion years). The global energy usage of our technological society is twenty times less than the current energy usage of the planet's microbial biomass ("The Living Cosmos" Professor Chris Impey).

The ratio of gases to one another in the Atmosphere has been relatively constant for a long time due to many feedback loops. For example, increased carbon dioxide in the atmosphere results in a flush of vegetative growth, which in turn removes carbon dioxide (increased organic matter, this carbon can eventually end up back in the atmosphere due to microbial activity breaking down organic matter).

The increased temperature results in more microbial activity. Microbial activity increases rock weathering (erosion); rock particles take up carbonate to form calcium carbonate (limestone), which eventually settles on the seafloor to form limestone, thereby reducing atmospheric CO2. This carbon may end up back in the atmosphere due to limestone entering the molten magma and being ejected as carbon dioxide as a result of volcanic eruptions.)

Both these feedback loops counteract global warming; however may not be able to counteract our increasing carbon dioxide production. Impey states that our industrial society may be shifting the equilibrium too far. I am not sure if climate scientists can understand how all the variables will play out; however, we cannot risk it.

Just to add to the confusion, there are issues such as the effect of cloud cover, the Milankovich cycles (Orbital flexing where the earth gets closer to the sun every ninety thousand years plus the orbital axis tilting cycle every forty-one thousand years) and the El Nino /La Nina cycles (four-to- twelve-year ocean current change). However, these issues are short- and-long-term cycles and are irrelevant to the steady temperature buildup due to increasing carbon dioxide.

Natural feedback loops will assist in delaying global warming. I suspect that industrialization is so extensive and happening so fast as to outstrip the ability of natural feedback loops to counteract the CO2 and temperature rise. I also suspect that the most likely situation is that the planet cannot sustain significantly higher levels of atmospheric greenhouse gases without a runaway greenhouse effect. Unlike the ancient atmosphere, the sun has become more intense over time, reducing the amount of leeway we have. We should be prudent, as advanced life may be so rare as to be unique to this planet. However, we should not assume that things are unchanging like our predecessors assumed earth bounty was inexhaustive.

Buying carbon credits off a third-world nation that would not cut down the forest anyway will achieve nothing. Likewise, world leaders committing to reducing carbon emissions to pre-industrial levels without understanding how it is even possible will achieve nothing. Expensive alternative energy schemes, without ensuring baseload energy requirements are maintained, will not do it.

The above solutions make people feel good. Let's instead be realistic, recognise the size of the problem, and realize that if our living standards are to be maintained. Society continues to advance; our energy requirements will continue to increase. I can see no current viable, cost-effective alternative to the nuclear energy solution. Still, I do realise that my knowledge and imagination limit this line of thought.

The pastoral farming industry is being targeted with emissions taxes. Grass removes carbon dioxide as it grows. It is consumed by livestock, which produces carbon dioxide and methane. Atmospheric methane breaks down into carbon dioxide; grass takes up carbon dioxide (a closed-loop, I would have thought). It's better than that. Grass decays quickly. As a result, the humus level (topsoil depth, a carbon store) increases over time. Pastoral farming may be a carbon sink.

I understand that Professor Alex McBratney of Sydney University has been researching the significance of soil systems as a carbon sink. Soil carbon sequestration is a complex issue and depends on factors such as the time of year and rainfall. The Kyoto agreement considers pastoral farming to be a methane source. Feedlot farming, widely practised in the Northern Hemisphere, is a carbon source, whereas pastoral farming is a carbon sink. I believe Kyoto is all about redistributing wealth from some nations to others. Northern hemisphere nations would not wish their agricultural sector to be disadvantaged.

It seems strange to me that government is targeting the private sector when this sector is more efficient. State sector waste is a source of carbon emissions. There is much that the state could do if the will to do so existed. An example is local body landfills. Methane is supposedly a much more severe greenhouse gas than carbon dioxide. Local bodies bury waste in landfills where it decomposes, producing copious quantities of methane. In Japan, the practice is to incinerate waste in incinerators. The heat is used to produce steam to power a steam turbine for electricity production. Two things are achieved: carbon dioxide is produced instead of methane, and electricity is a by-product.

If carbon emissions are to be reduced, target unproductive waste in the state sector and large power generators. Don't take the easy option of taxing the efficient private sector because this is simply suppressing the economy. We need a lot of energy to grow our economy, and we need a lot of electricity if we are to charge up electric cars and produce hydrogen for hydrogen-powered vehicles.

We should investigate nuclear power as an option. It has been safely used by the world's largest democracies for electricity generation, for fifty years now. It is safe, and there are no carbon emissions. Instead, Kyoto means we are subsidizing nuclear power production elsewhere.

Let us look at the alternatives to using fossil fuels for the bulk of the world's energy supply. Currently, many nations are reliant on coal and gas for electricity production. This is particularly so in Australia (S.A and Tasmania excepted). Tasmania is fortunate enough to use hydro as its baseload source. South Australia is trying to use wind (unsuccessfully, I believe, as South Australia is still reliant on baseload electricity from other states).

Solar and wind are the two main renewable energies being promoted. Wind generation is expensive. Massive towers are being built, but they are not cheap, and each supports a fairly small generator. So what happens when there is no wind or sunlight (a still night)?

South Australia imports power from Victoria and N.S.W.

Let's ask another question: what does this entail? It requires coal-fired power stations in these states to be on standby. A coal-fired powered station cannot be turned on at the flick of a switch; a furnace needs to be kept hot if it is on standby. It takes days to bring a cold furnace online without destroying the brick refractory. How is this helping us achieve a low carbon emission future?

People talk about storage devices and the fact that battery technology is improving. No person can predict future technology. Based on my current knowledge, I cannot see how it is practical to store energy (for heavy industry and cities) using batteries, hot liquid storage tanks, etc. The best continuous baseload sources of low carbon energy for electricity production are geothermal and hydro. New Zealand produces almost 100 per cent of its electricity using these sources. Australia is a flat dry country with few significant river systems. Australia is not geophysically active, so it cannot tap into underground steam. Australia must look elsewhere.

Nuclear fission reactors have been around since the 1950s. However, it is well-proven technology that has not received widespread support in many nations due to safety concerns and what some would call a widespread paranoid concern due to a lack of understanding of radiation.

The greens are opposed to the free enterprise system and nuclear energy. So let's look at the consequences.

Human density—It has long been speculated that we are running out of resources. I will quote from "The Case for Space" by Robert Zubrin. "Two hundred years ago, the English economist, Thomas Malthus, proposed that population growth must always outrun production as a fundamental law of nature. In fact, over the two centuries since Malthus wrote, the world population has risen seven-fold while inflation-adjusted gross domestic product per capita has increased by a factor of fifty. Indeed, it is clear the Malthusian argument is fundamentally nonsense. Resources are a function of technology, the more people there are and the higher their living standard, the more inventors, and thus inventions there will be and the faster the resource base will expand. It is human ingenuity that turns natural raw materials into resources. Uranium and thorium were not resources till we invented nuclear power. Twenty years ago, shale oil was not a resource. Today, because of the invention of new horizontal drilling and fracking techniques, it's an enormous resource. So the fact of the matter is that humanity is not running out of resources. On the contrary, we are exponentially expanding our resources. We can do so because the true source of resources is not the earth, ocean, or the sky. It is human creativity". I believe planet earth could support ten times our current population of 7.5 billion more minor less environmental than today. The solution is density: energy density, agricultural density, and population concentration. Energy density—Let's ignore concerns over the safety of nuclear for the time being. Safety concerns are covered later. Uranium is a dense source of energy. I understand that to cater to the additional electricity requirements of the planet over the next twenty years would need to cover a land area the size of Russia with evenly spaced wind turbines. Then we will still need an equal amount of backup. A good source to explain the issue is "Apocalypse Never" – Michael Shellenberger

Agricultural density—I once owned a controlled environment greenhouse. Hydroponics means you provide the specific nutrients for the particular crop (something that cannot be achieved in soil). Adding specific bacteria to your nutrient solution enhances the ability of plants to take up the nutrients and can be used to crowd pathogens in the root zone. The plant hormone auxin can also be added to improve root development. Humidity regulation reduces fungal disease. Integrated pest control (Using good bugs to kill nasty bugs) controls pests (pesticides are not used in many modern greenhouses). Temperature control optimizes growth (and in some cases, artificial lighting and CO_2 enhancement increases yield). The capital cost of modern greenhouses is high, but so are the yields. Modern cities could feed themselves if such greenhouses were placed on rooftops. The limiting factor is energy; a lot of energy is needed.

It should now be apparent to the reader how population density can increase in some localities while reducing pressure on wilderness areas. We need lots of energy for desalination plants, electrifying rail, a move towards electric cars, etc. If space travel becomes a reality using existing technology, mankind will need a massive amount of energy. Energy to make rocket fuel. Electrolysis to split water molecules into hydrogen and oxygen. Energy combines atmospheric CO_2 and water to make methane (global warming neutral, made from CO_2 and water, then back to CO_2 and water when it burns). It takes more energy to manufacture rocket fuel than the energy contained in it. There may be ongoing resistance towards nuclear. However, it is safe and the only option. Much said about Chernobyl is factually incorrect; there is no evidence that more than 62 people died due to radiation (cancer, radiation sickness). I do not know the motivation behind all the sensationalistic nonsense; it is frustrating. Nuclear fission reactors have been around since the 1950s. It is a well-proven technology. However, it has not received widespread support in many nations due to safety concerns and what some would call a widespread paranoid concern due to a lack of understanding of what radiation is. It has been assumed by the World Health Organization and other groups that any level of ionizing radiation is hazardous and that there is a linear relationship between ionizing radiation exposure and cancer rates. For this reason, the safe limit for ionizing radiation has been set very low, marginally above the background level of this radiation. There is a background level; our bodies are constantly exposed to this category of radiation emanating from radioactive sources in the ground and elsewhere.

Living cells lived in and evolved in a much higher radiation environment earlier in the earth's history. Background radiation speeds up the evolutionary process by mutating DNA, thereby increasing genetic variation. Cells also evolved techniques for combating radiation; cells evolved in a much higher background radiation environment than currently exists on this planet. According to Impey in *The Living Cosmos,* "Some of life's earliest evolutionary advances included mechanisms to repair DNA and deal with radiation damage. Examples include lateral gene transfer and meiosis. Bacteria have had advanced methods for repairing DNA for three billion years" (160).

There is a school of thought that slightly elevated levels (above the current background level) of ionizing radiation may reduce cancer rates.

The following quotes are from "Radiation Hormesis: Historical Perspective and implications for low-Dose Cancer Risk Assessment".

The references can be found online at ***www.ncbi.nlm.nih. gov/PMC/articles/PMC2889502/***

"It was repeatedly shown that low dose rates activate a system of co-operative protection processes in the body. They were found to promote intracellular and intercellular signalling pathways, that leads to activated natural protection against cancer" (Luckey 2003; Prekeges 2003;

Schollnberger et al. 2004; Feinendegen 2005; Scott and Di Palma 2007; Feinendegen et al. 2007; Liu 2007; Scott et al. 2007 2009). "Mortality of British Radiologists who had registered since 1954 was remarkably low in comparison to medical practitioners as a whole; this was true for both cancer and all other causes of death combined" (Berrington et al. 2001). Cameron (2002) stressed that the British radiology data showed that moderate doses are beneficial rather than a risk to health."

"A Canadian study examining the effect of occupational exposure among nuclear industry workers found that cancer mortality among this population was 58% of the national average" (Abbatt et al. 1983)."

"In the United Kingdom, a negative association between radiation exposure and mortality from cancers was found for radiation workers (Kendall et al. 1992)". It appears that slightly elevated levels of radiation are beneficial to health, but levels above 100 mSv, the risk appears to increase as the bodies natural defence mechanisms are overwhelmed. Based on an analysis of the data of Thompson et al. (2008), lifetime exposure to residential radon at a level of 4 pCi/l of air appears to be associated with a 60 per cent reduction in lung cancer cases (Scott et al. 2009). At Fukushima, one person died inside the building when a plant fell on him during the earthquake. To date, zero (yes zero) people died from radiation sickness. There is no evidence that the cancer rate has increased.

The following two quotes are from "Fear vs. Radiation: The Mismatch," *NY Times*; *http://www.nytimes. com/2013/10/22/opinion/fear-vs-radiation-the-mismatch. html*."

"Beginning shortly after World War 2, epidemiologists and radiation biologists began tracking atomic bomb survivors. Researchers have followed roughly 112,600 Japanese: 86,611 who had been within 10 kilometres of the centre of the explosions and 26,000 who were not exposed. The most current analysis estimates that, out of 10,929 people in the exposed population who have died of cancer, only 527 of those deaths were caused by radiation from the atomic bombs. For the entire population exposed, in many cases to extremely high radiation levels, that is an excess cancer mortality rate of about two-thirds of one per cent. These studies have also found that, more than two generations later, there have been no intergenerational genetic effects on humans"."Perhaps most importantly, research on the bomb survivors has found that at lower doses, below 100 millisieverts, radiation causes no detectable elevations in normal rates of illness or disease. The vast majority of the doses received by people living near Fukushima and Chernobyl were well below this one hundred millisievert level. The robust evidence that ionizing radiation is a relatively low health risk dramatically contradicts common fears". Nuclear energy is the only realistic option for baseload power that does not result in CO2 emissions. The best option, I believe, is one hundred per cent nuclear, not a mix of energy sources. There is an argument for solar stations on outback cattle stations, otherwise trying to have a mix of energy sources only adds to the cost. It will take a very long time to make the transition. The number one environmental concern at the moment is global warming. It is good to have a basic understanding of how things are happening. A reason why there are so many sceptics could be because there has not been an adequate attempt at explaining the issues to the public. The attitude is that science is too complex, yet it can be explained in simplistic terms. The common argument against global warming is that infrared in the required wavelengths can only travel ten meters, on average, before interacting with CO_2. Therefore saturation has already been attained. The saturation rebuttal is flawed. The problem is that CO_2 creates resistance, i.e., Photons are taken up by CO_2 molecules then re-emitted, slowing the energy pathway to space.

The energy coming into the system will always equate to what is radiating back into space. Imagine a barrel with two slats missing. If you pour water into that barrel, the water level will rise till the water leaving equates with that entering. The water level represents temperature and the two missing slats resistance. Increase resistance by replacing one of the two missing slats. The water level doubles till the water in equals water out. In this example, the water level represents temperature. It does not matter that all the infrared in the correct spectrum already interacts with CO_2; it is the resistance to the movement towards space that is the issue. The temperature of the whole system increases before the new equilibrium is reached. Global warming could be happening; I keep changing my mind (some people never change their minds over some issues; however, it is a good thing to change your mind, it means you are taking on board new information). Regardless, it is not a good idea to keep increasing atmospheric CO_2. I understand that CO_2 was lower than at any time in history (and still is). CO_2 levels are so low (0.04%) that plant growth is being restricted. The planet coped with levels five times higher 200 million years ago. The wild card is that the sun was 1% cooler back then. Our sun is beginning to fuse heavier elements as it heads towards red giant status. I am not a supporter of the cataclysmic climate change scenario however believe we need to be prudent.

A better-structured society will enable us to do incredible things. Western nations should have achieved a growth rate similar to China's; instead, we chose a path of self-doubt, regulations, and big brother government.

There may be trillions of stars in the observable universe. They are located in the 200-400 billion galaxies estimated to be observable to us (a more recent survey suggests the figure may be in the trillions). There are more stars than the total of grains of sand on every beach on this planet. It appears most stars have solar systems of many planets. Yet, we may be alone.

If we are alone, then it is only us who can contemplate the Universe. Humans only can give meaning to it. Our small, vulnerable planet may be unique in the vastness of the cosmos. We must survive and expand life into the great beyond.It is easy to be green. You simply oppose everything, dams, nuclear, fossil fuels, the free enterprise system, whatever. Yet, many people (probably most people) out there are as concerned about the environment as the most rabid green but do not support the green movement. They recognise that you cannot turn back the clock without dire consequences. They recognise that sometimes it is necessary to choose the best from many undesirable choices. We need more than simple opposition; we need solutions. We need to look at the big picture; people need a deeper understanding of the issues. People need more excellent knowledge; we need better media reporting. Restrictions imposed because of superficial beliefs can have unintended consequences.

Plutonium, a fission by-product, is not waste. It can be reused in later generation power plants and produce many times the energy obtained from the original uranium. As a result, existing fission fuel would produce our current electricity needs for a thousand years. (I expect a lot less as our energy needs increase, but fission gives mankind a reprieve.)

We live on a radioactive planet. The background radiation is high and exists everywhere. (I hope you are not paranoid.) The reason our planet's core is not solid is because of ongoing energy released from radioactive materials within the mantra since the planet's formation.

Australia has 40 per cent of the world's known minable uranium reserves. (If we stop digging it up and selling it to the rest of the world at a below-market price, we could be the future Saudi Arabia of the world.) Nuclear waste is not an issue if stored underground in a safe location (after all, the uranium came out of the ground in the first place). Australia is geologically the safest place in the world for waste storage. Almost all of Australia's electricity is produced in coal-fired power stations. Australia has high electricity consumption relative to our population, in part due to the mineral smelting industry. Solar and wind generation are expensive. A very costly wind turbine would not produce much more electricity than a $5000 Chinese diesel generator. We would bankrupt our nation trying to adopt these technologies as an alternative to our significant current generators.

Because The voting public will resist nuclear, major power generation has been placed in the "too hard" basket. Instead, the Government chooses to establish a punitive carbon regime on the private sector (the carbon tax has since been abandoned), a misplaced regime, especially regarding pastoral farming. The current proposals will only slow down economic growth.

Australia should gradually move towards nuclear electricity production. There should be sound debate over nuclear waste storage. The Great Artesian Basin covers 1.7 million square kilometres or 22 per cent of the continent. I am sure that this reservoir is already in contact with more naturally occurring radioactive material in the rock structure than what could be stored as waste. However, any waste can be rendered safe so that it does not leach and also areas where there is subterranean water can be avoided. If radioactive materials are stored in a localized area, I doubt there would be much natural movement from that site even after ten thousand years. Currently, unsafe spent radioactive material (from hospitals and industry) is stored in our cities due to irrational opposition to a storage facility. Such a storage faculty should primarily be for Australia's waste. If any waste is transported to Australia, this should only be after rendering, and containment has made that material almost 100 per cent safe. If a mishap should occur (e.g., a ship sinking), then there should be no environmental risk. A government's first responsibility is the safety of its citizens.

I have since read Dr Bernardine Atkinson's book *Ecological Sustainability and the Nuclear Power Story*" (Trafford Publishing 2010). The nuclear situation is even better than I imagined. Uranium-235 may be non-renewable, but its by-products (such as plutonium) will be able to supply the world (at current energy consumption) electricity via nuclear fission for more than one thousand years. A very safe energy source, no CO_2 emissions, a cheap energy source, are we crazy? Please read Dr Bernardine's book. We have been misled and are missing out on the benefits of a valuable resource.

The future will be a nuclear one; we cannot continue down the present path. All sorts of excuses for not pursuing a nuclear future in Australia are being made. One is that we do not have the expertise. Then what is the excuse for not reopening the nuclear science school that once existed at Sydney University?

If we have low carbon emission and inexpensive (yes, in the long run, nuclear is less expensive than coal) electricity, then we can increase electricity production even further, thereby making further carbon dioxide emission reductions by substituting electricity for other fossil fuels (electrifying rail, only allowing electric cars into the CBD of cities etc.), positive steps towards reducing carbon emissions. In addition, desalination plants can take pressure off the Murry-Darling basin.

The Earths microbial biomass (total of all single-celled microbes) have been partly (along with plants) been responsible for regulating the planet's oxygen: carbon dioxide ratio. The following are some interesting facts (obtained from Impey @The Living Cosmos@) about the planet's microbial biomass.

- The global energy usage of our technological society is twenty times less than the current energy usage of the planets microbial biomass".
- Microbes make up 90 per cent of the planet's biomass.
- Our oceans should be very saline due to rock weathering but has maintained a salinity of 3.4 per cent salt concentration. Chris Impey states, "There is still no good model for how ocean salinity is regulated. However, it must be relevant that bacteria make up one-third of the oceans' biomass and 80 per cent of its biological active surface area due to their high surface-area-to-volume ratio. Plus, they pump salt."

- Some bacteria can live in extreme conditions.
- Bacillus infernus was found because of deep drilling in Virginia. Lives in rock three miles below the surface. It has no access to oxygen and instead uses iron and manganese dioxide for respiration.
- Deinococcus radiodurans was discovered when a can of irradiated food was still spoiled even after irradiation. This bacteria can tolerate radiation thousands of times more intense than a dose that would kill a human. In addition, it has an amazing ability to repair damage to its DNA.
- Thermophile bacteria can live and grow in superheated water (above 100 degrees) around thermal vents.

A human body can contain 100 trillion foreign or microbial cells (throughout the entire body, not just the gut). This means 90 per cent of the body's cells are nonhuman microbes. The symbiotic relationship between the cells of our bodies and trillions of microbes spans vast periods starting with the first microbes over 3.5 billion years ago. Only recently, the importance of the body's microbiome has been recognised (Chopra and Tanzi, *Super Genes* 2015 p108). So maybe another good reason to limit antibiotic use in emergencies (apart from limiting pathogen resistance) is to avoid harming symbiotic bacteria in the body.

I'd like to mention littering and plastic at this time. Plastic compacts down reasonably well in landfills. It compacts down to a relatively small percentage of the landfill content. Also, more importantly, it is inert; it does not leach toxic chemicals (unlike, among other things, paper). However, plastic is a concern when people litter. It is unsightly, can be ingested by stock, and ultimately washes out to sea, endangering marine life. In chapter 6, I discussed zero tolerance for petty crimes such as graffiti. Littering is a petty crime; perhaps the zero-tolerance policy should apply. Also, substantial penalties should apply (In Singapore, defiant litterers can be expected to clean up a specified area while wearing a bright luminous green vest. One aim is to shame the offender publicly). People should accept responsibility for their actions.

It would be great if what I have written results in broadening some people's outlook. None of what I have written is a solution in isolation. There are seven billion people out there, each with their thoughts. It would be great if people looked at things from a big picture perspective. It is easy to be a greeny. You simply oppose everything-dams, nuclear energy, fossil fuels, whatever. Yet there are many people (probably most people) are as concerned about the environment as the most rabid greeny but do not support the green movement. They recognise that you cannot turn back the clock without dire consequences. They recognise that sometimes it is necessary to choose the best from several undesirable choices. We need more than simple opposition; we need solutions. We need to look at the big picture; people need a deeper understanding of the issues. People need greater knowledge; we need better media reporting. Restrictions imposed because of superficial beliefs can have unintended consequences.

CHAPTER 8

THE FUTURE

People cannot predict future technology. It comes at us from unexpected directions. Where, for instance, is this future that will prevent CO2 emissions and supply our energy needs? No person can be sure. However, the fear of the unknown could be our greatest threat.

Let us outline one possible future which may sound farfetched but is being taken very seriously by both private organizations and NASA.

A satellite at an altitude of about thirty-five thousand kilometres is in Geo-stationary orbit. It will sit above the same part of the earth by completing a complete orbit in one day. Any object which sits above a point on the ground but is below this altitude will fall to the ground; its centrifugal force throwing it outwards is less than the gravitational pull. Any likewise object that is above the geostationary altitude will be thrown away from the planet. If a cable anchored to the ground stretched to an altitude of more than double geostationary orbit, say to one hundred thousand kilometres, it would stay in position as the centrifugal force on the cable will be greater than the gravitational pull. This idea has been around for some time but relegated to science fantasy as no known material would be strong enough (a steel cable would simply snap due to its weight). The material would need to be 180 times the strength of steel. Very recently, technology has resulted in the concept being resurrected.

During the 1990s, a new form of carbon, a carbon nanotube, was discovered. Carbon nanotubes have a strength, weight for weight, of 400 times that of steel. One of the discoverers was the late Richard Smalley, who won a Noble prize in 1996 for his research. A Dr Bradley Edwards has developed the idea further. It is now believed to be possible to stitch carbon nanotubes together into a continuous ribbon. It is considered that it may be possible to place a thin cable in place by setting a twenty-tonne satellite into geostationary orbit, then unwinding the cable. The cable can then be strengthened by climbing elevators to stitch more fibre onto the existing cable. The elevators would be electrically powered, the energy source being an infrared energy beam from the ground. All of a sudden, space looks accessible, ground-based space rockets being leapfrogged (redundant). The best location for this cable is a platform off the coast of Western Australia. This location is outside the orbit of most space junk and a region with few storms. Western Australia could become the gateway to space. There are still major technical issues, such as likely static build-up in the cable. The concept is no longer considered practical but is an example of how unexpected concepts can develop.

This could lead to large but affordable orbiting solar power stations which use lightweight foil on a lightweight structure to form a parabola to focus light on a collector. This energy could then be sent to the ground via an infrared beam. Maybe the moon could be mined for a material found in the Apollo moon rocks. Helium 3, rare on this planet, is common on the moon's surface due to being baked by solar gamma rays for billions of years. Helium 3 is what is needed to make nuclear fusion power stations practical (combining atoms instead of splitting them as in nuclear fission).

As for the great questions, we may never know the answers. Did the universe start from a point in time and space, as the big bang theory suggests? The recent discovery that the universe is expanding at an accelerating rate has suggested that the known universe is part of something larger. We know that there are more than a billion stars in many galaxies. We know that there are billions of galaxies in the known universe. We have found large planets circling nearby stars. We know Einstein's theory of relativity holds up. We do not know if another life exists out there. Could other intelligent civilizations exist, but the distances are so great that they will never come into contact? Are we unique? Is the probability of self-replicating molecules being produced in an organic soup and then those molecules evolving into primitive cells so unlikely? These are questions we may never know the answers to. Will the human species ever reach out into the great beyond? This we also cannot be sure of. We have two options, push on a full flight with technology while minimizing wastage and inefficiency, or else let our fears and self-doubts lead to a stagnant and ultimately declining society. I say, let's push on.

Who knows where the future will lead, but let us embrace the future, don't fight technology and economic growth on the assumption that we are running out of options because we're not.

The Great Beyond

Until now, the focus has been on the immediate future and how society needs to be restructured. First, let's talk about our place in the universe.

It has taken life 3.5 billion years to evolve from its beginnings to the present. Early life began not long after the formation of the planets. Life started on hot planet earth in an oxygen-deficient environment (oxygenation of the atmosphere came later with photosynthesis).

In about a half billion years, the earth will become uninhabitable as the sun increasingly fuses helium and heavier elements (due to hydrogen depletion) and heads towards red giant status. This means that our long-lived main-sequence star has given evolution just enough time to create intelligent life.

We don't know if we are alone. Intelligent life is likely so improbable that we are indeed alone. If you subscribe to the theory of evolution, you will probably agree that there is no reason we are here, we just evolved. Homo Sapiens owe it to three and a half billion years of evolution to make the leap off the planet and into the great beyond. It may be that the next fifty to one hundred years and how we organise our societies could be a critical phase in advance of life. This is something that is driving Elon Musk. His view is that we may only get one opportunity to become a spacefaring civilization, and that opportunity may be right now.

Stars are a temporary intermediate phase in the life of the universe. There are still billions of years left for our stellar universe as new stars are still forming from interstellar dust. Eventually, stars will die, one by one, as all available fuel for nuclear fusion is used up. After that, the universe will become dark and cold as it reaches maximum entropy.

Human knowledge is limited. We know that the known universe is like an inflating balloon. All galaxies are within this balloon (except take away the skin). The inflation started from the point of space and time and decelerated due to the gravitational pull between mass particles. The expansion eventually went from deceleration to acceleration. This is believed to be due to the gravitational effect of dark energy that comes out of nothing and is of uniform density. Many galaxies (including the Milky Way) have a massive black hole at their centre. Also, there are numerous smaller black holes scattered among the one hundred billion stars in our galaxy due to supernovae. More and more stars are falling into black holes; however, as the universe reaches maximum entropy, many stars will avoid this fate. They will simply become fading white dwarfs.

Physicists and astronomers can only talk about what is observable and testable. Who knows what knowledge will be acquired in the future. What is truly unique is that a species (Homo Sapiens) evolved and can speculate about such things.

CONCLUSION

Humankind has made massive technological advances over the last century, yet we have structures and institutions that have changed little and regulate and control every aspect of our lives. Regulations and legislation have been passed ad hoc to respond to the latest thinking or crisis. The challenge for the near future is to restructure our society, to remove self-imposed constraints on progress. We have become so constrained that we have moved away from the principles we hold dear: liberty and equality, and by the people, of the people, for the people—that is, personal empowerment.

The following is a model not just for Australia but for all nations. It is a summary of this book, and everything is based on two concepts. One is the concept of personal empowerment and responsibility. The other is the concept that competition and a level playing field results in efficiency, innovation, and ultimately growth. I believe that by adopting the model, Australia would achieve the sort of growth rate currently being experienced by emerging Asian economies. The result would be a happy, prosperous, low crime society. To achieve this, the government should

- Introduce stronger competition legislation to minimize the formation of monopolies and anticompetitive behaviour;
- Introduce privatization and competitive model for the state and private sectors;
- Legislative responsibility act, requiring new and existing legislation to go through a cost to society of compliance test;
- Introduce education accounts and school choice;
- Enact private health and Insurance-based model like Japan's;
- Consider nuclear energy as an alternative to coal-fired power production;
- Do not impose punitive carbon schemes on the private sector;
- Remove all protectionism—tariffs, subsidies, grants;
- Dump income tax, land tax, stamp duties—replace all with GST. remove all GST exemptions except on financial transactions;
- Introduce a universal basic income scheme.
- Dump Federal system; dump state governments, just one democratically elected legislative chamber for all of Australia;
- Enact tougher sentencing for convicted criminals;
- Begin mentoring programs;
- Remove baby bonuses;
- Consider lifetime dole limits;
- Emphasize shared parenting with provisos; and

- Reinstate the Privy Council (or similar international appeal court).

Such a model would result in a substantial increase in GDP growth (and personal income growth). Of course, no country has all the components described in place, but it is all achievable.

The reality with restructuring is that there is pain before gain. It takes many years before an economy responds favourably. In the meantime, all that can be seen is the pain. The magnitude of restructuring suggested in this book would result in the loss of thousands of state sector jobs. A loss of jobs of this magnitude could initially cause a small economic downturn due to reduced spending. The private sector could not place all the redundant personnels till the inevitable economic expansion occurred. The incumbent government will crash in the popularity stakes. This is a problem with democracy; the only solution is getting the message out, education and communication. It is a failing of the media.

Those in a privileged position will defend their privileges. However, they will not see the big picture, which is that they may be better off if privileges are also removed from other groups.

How can the restructuring be done as humanely as possible? Should it be done gradually over time or quickly so that the gains begin to flow sooner?

Gradual change will not work unless the main political parties have the same understanding. Traditionally, a change of government results in the previous government's reforms being unwound. I have an uneasy feeling that the world is reaching a turning point; we may no longer have time to pussyfoot around. The restructuring will lead to a high growth prosperous nation. The problem is undertaking the reforms and how to complete the process as humanely as possible. Is doing nothing an alternative? I don't think so. I hope that this restructuring phase is not impossible. I know that we have an inefficient oversized state sector, excessive regulations, significant social problems, and a mindset that resists deviation from the status quo.

Members of Parliament are there to work for me/us, not control me/us. You have not been placed there to follow a particular party ideology or dogma blindly. You are there to do what you honestly believe is right. For this reason, I do not care if an MP changes parties or crosses the floor as long as they are following their convictions rather than blindly following an ideology. I want from politicians what works. If you are honest and look at examples worldwide, excessive government and central planning have not worked long term.

There is no doubt that the future is scary. If you subscribe to the theory of evolution, you will agree that the human species is now evolving backwards. Due to modern society and medical science, more and more people may be passing on genetic problems (all genetic variations are now perpetuated). This is an issue I do not like thinking about (there appears to be no solution that does not infringe fundamental rights and our ethics), but it confronts us.

Fear of the future is no reason for impeding economic and social development. That is a recipe for disaster. The world's population is too large; we have moved too far, we will have no future without further technological advancement and economic growth.

The purpose of this book is to publicize an economic and social alternative that is already well known to classic liberals around the world. With any concept, more publicity leads to more people embracing it. Eventually, a tipping point is reached where more and more people hear about and support a concept. This can ultimately lead to the concept's adoption.

In recent times there has been a feeling of hopelessness that society is reaching a precipice. This has been brought on by a combination of economic stagnation and a lack of technological progress in certain areas, especially in energy production and space technology.

I have become conscious of my mortality. A question I am sure everyone asks at some time is, "What is the purpose of our short existence?" Maybe most people's legacy is in some way to contribute a very small amount towards the steady advancement of humanity. The degree of satisfaction that this goal is being achieved depends on whether society appears to be advancing.

Society has an exciting future if only we are prepared to grasp it. We must allow people to achieve their full potential. We must unleash the shackles of taxation, excessive regulation, and state control. If only we would do so, then we would be on a fast elevator to the future. If only.

BIBLIOGRAPHY

"Wealth and Poverty"	George Gilder	Institute for Contemporary Studies, San Fransisco 1993
"Future Wealth"	Francis McInerney and Sean White	St Martins Press 2000
"The Law"	Frederic Bastiat	Institute for Liberal Values. N.Z.

REFERENCES

"Wealth and Poverty"	George Gilder	Institute for Contemporary Studies, San Fransisco 1993
"The Great Boom Ahead"	Harry S Dent	Griffin Paperbacks, Adelaide 1993
Roaring 2000s Investor	Harry S Dent	Touchstone 1230 Avenue, New York 1999
"Future Wealth"	Francis McInerney and Sean White	St Martins Press 2000
"The Law"	Frederic Bastiat	Institute for Liberal Values. N.Z.
"Leaving the Planet	Bradley C Edwards Ph. D.	
By Space Elevator"	Philip Ragan	Lulu.com Seattle

"Let Parents Choose"	Deborah Coddington 2002	The Valentine Press, P.O. Box 99-075, Newmarket, Auckland 1031 N.Z.
"Closing the Gaps"		ACT NZ Parliamentary Office 2001
"Unfinished Business"	Sir Roger Douglas	Random House NZ Ltd 1993
"The Case for Space"	Robert Zubrin	Prometheus Books 2019
"Apocalypse Never"	Michael Shellenberger	Harper 2020
"Entrepreneurship"	John G Burch	John Wiley and Sons INC 1986 p 19
"Ecological sustainability and the Nuclear Power Story"	Dr Bernardine Atkinson 2009	www.digitalprintaustralia.com
"Radiation Hormesis: Historical Perspective and implications for low-Dose Cancer Risk Assessment"	Alexander M Vaiserman	www.ncbi.nlm.nih.gov/pmc/articles/PMC2889502/

"Fear vs Radiation: The Mismatch"	David Ropeik	The New York Times Oct. 21, 2013
"The Living Cosmos"	Chris Impey	Cambridge University Press 2007
"Super Genes"	Deepak Chopra and Rudolph E. Tanzi	Random House 2015